A Closer Look at

PLANT CLASSIFICATIONS, PARTS, AND USES

A Closer Look at

PLANT CLASSIFICATIONS, PARTS, AND USES

Edited by Sherman Hollar

Britannica
Educational Publishing
IN ASSOCIATION WITH
ROSEN
EDUCATIONAL SERVICES

Published in 2012 by Britannica Educational Publishing
(a trademark of Encyclopædia Britannica, Inc.)
in association with Rosen Educational Services, LLC
29 East 21st Street, New York, NY 10010.

Distributed exclusively by Rosen Educational Services.
For a listing of additional Britannica Educational Publishing titles, call toll free (800) 237-9932.

First Edition

Britannica Educational Publishing
Michael I. Levy: Executive Editor, Encyclopædia Britannica
J.E. Luebering: Director, Core Reference Group, Encyclopædia Britannica
Adam Augustyn: Assistant Manager, Encyclopædia Britannica

Anthony L. Green: Editor, Compton's by Britannica
Michael Anderson: Senior Editor, Compton's by Britannica
Sherman Hollar: Associate Editor, Compton's by Britannica

Marilyn L. Barton: Senior Coordinator, Production Control
Steven Bosco: Director, Editorial Technologies
Lisa S. Braucher: Senior Producer and Data Editor
Yvette Charboneau: Senior Copy Editor
Kathy Nakamura: Manager, Media Acquisition

Rosen Educational Services
Heather M. Moore Niver: Editor
Nelson Sá: Art Director
Cindy Reiman: Photography Manager
Karen Huang: Photo Researcher
Matthew Cauli: Designer, Cover Design
Introduction by Heather M. Moore Niver

Library of Congress Cataloging-in-Publication Data

A closer look at plant classifications, parts, and uses / edited by Sherman Hollar.—1st ed.
    p. cm.—(Introduction to biology)
"In association with Britannica Educational Publishing, Rosen Educational Services."
Includes bibliographical references and index.
ISBN 978-1-61530-529-2 (library binding)
1. Plants—Classification—Juvenile literature. 2. Plant anatomy—Juvenile literature. 3. Plants,
Useful—Juvenile literature. I. Hollar, Sherman.
QK95.C56 2012
571.3'2—dc22

2011008269

Manufactured in the United States of America

On the cover: A closeup of Frangipani silhouetted on a vista of late summer flowers. *Shutterstock.com*

Interior background images Shutterstock.com

CONTENTS

INTRODUCTION

The next time you eat breakfast, take a good look at the food on the table. Juice from an orange, buckwheat and blueberries in your pancakes, sweet maple syrup drizzled on top, and cocoa in your hot chocolate: all these items come from plants. In this book you will learn about what defines a plant and the different kinds of plants. You will learn about the parts of a plant, right down to its cells and tissues, and discover many uses of plants in our daily lives.

So what is a plant? Sure, we know that a maple tree is a kind of plant and a fish is not, but botanists (scientists who study plants) continue to debate the exact definition. For years scientists deemed an organism a plant if it had green pigment, could synthesize its own food with light, and was not mobile. All other organisms were regarded as part of the animal kingdom.

Closer studies of certain so-called plants revealed that they were not all that similar to plants and had a vastly different evolution. One basic characteristic of plants is that they are multicellular organisms that perform photosynthesis. Another is that the cell walls of plant cells contain a stiffening material known as cellulose, which makes tree trunks and twigs rigid. Plants are also recognized as eukaryotes, which means that their cells have a nucleus.

Plants are commonly organized by how they grow. Trees, shrubs, and herbs each grow differently and take distinct forms. Flowering plants can also be divided into a trio of classes based on their life cycle and growth pattern. Annuals complete their life cycle in one year, whereas biennials need two years. Perennials grow for more than two years. Finally, plants can be grouped according to their complexity. Nonvascular plants include liverworts, hornworts, and mosses. Seedless vascular plants include ferns and their relatives. Among vascular seed plants are conifers and flowering plants.

Cells make up every living thing, and in plants the cells come together to form tissues. Simple plant tissues (or ground tissues) are made up of only one type of cells. Simple tissues include parenchyma, collenchyma, and sclerenchyma tissues. Complex tissues— dermal and vascular—are composed of two or more types of cells.

At first glance plants might seem like pretty simple organisms, but further study reveals how complex they can be. Leaves

The passion-flower blossom (family Passifloraceae) displays a striking combination of sepals, petals, and stamens. Shutterstock.com

help make the plant's food by collecting sunlight. Stems give the plant support. The roots anchor the plant to the ground, draw water from the soil, and store food. Flowers, seeds, and fruits are part of the plant's reproductive system.

With some 270,000 different kinds of plants in existence (and possibly another

30,000 that have yet to be identified), these organisms play a significant role in our lives. Cereals and grains are a major source of our nutrition, and many livestock subsist on grains and grass as well. Cotton is a source of material for clothing, but did you know that synthetic fabrics like rayon are made from cellulose? Paper comes from plants. Many types of buildings and furniture are made from wood. Cork, rubber, and even cocoa butter also come from trees. Plants improve our atmosphere and provide us with fuel. In addition, plants of all kinds have been used in medicine. Foxglove, for example, produces digitalis, which helps treat heart disease.

Get ready to learn a lot about the incredibly diverse world of plants. These are complex, fascinating organisms that we could not do without.

CHAPTER 1

CHARACTERISTICS OF PLANTS

Wherever there is sunlight, air, and soil, plants can be found. On the northernmost coast of Greenland, the Arctic poppy peeps out from beneath the ice. Mosses and tussock grasses grow in Antarctica. Flowers of vivid color and great variety force their way up through

The Arctic poppy can bloom even under barren conditions.
Shutterstock.com

the snow on mountainsides. Many shrubs and cacti thrive in deserts that go without rain for years at a time, and rivers, lakes, and swamps are filled with water plants.

The scientists who study plants— botanists—have named and described approximately 270,000 different kinds of plants. They estimate that another 30,000 unidentified species exist in less explored ecosystems such as tropical forests.

PLANTS AND THE BALANCE OF NATURE

Plants are essential parts of ecosystems. Most of the energy consumed in terrestrial ecosystems is provided by plants, and as a consequence, land animals are dependent on them for their food. Plants absorb minerals, such as potassium and phosphorus, from the soil. These are stored in plant tissues and are an essential part of the diet of animals that eat plants. Plants help form, enrich, and sta-bilize soil. Hearty mosses help break down and crumble rock into soil. The roots of trees and other plants also contribute to this process. Decaying plant material such as leaves increases the fertility of soil. Plant roots hold the soil in place and prevent erosion.

WHAT DISTINGUISHES PLANTS FROM OTHER LIVING THINGS?

Exactly what is a plant and how is it different from other life-forms? Initially, this may seem like a simple question. Everyone knows that an elm tree is a plant, whereas a dog is not. Nevertheless, the precise definition of plants is still a matter of debate among some scientists.

As recently as the late 1960s, scientists believed that all organisms could be classified as members of either the plant or the animal kingdom. Life-forms that are green and that can synthesize their own food using light energy were put in the plant kingdom. Those organisms that lack green pigment and are able to move about were considered to be animals. As scientists made more detailed studies of certain organisms that were considered to be plants, they recognized that they were quite different from plants and that they did not share an evolutionary history with them.

Herbivores like horses get many minerals from plants. Hemera/Thinkstock

Today plants are recognized as multi-cellular organisms that carry out photosynthesis. This activity takes place in special structures, or organelles, called chloroplasts and makes use of a green chemical compound called chlorophyll. Another important characteristic of plant cells is that they have cell walls that are composed of cellulose, the stiffening material in tree trunks, twigs, and the veins of leaves.

Plants are eukaryotes—that is, their cells contain a true nucleus and other membrane-bound bodies. This property distinguishes plants from bacteria and archaea, which are prokaryotes—organisms made up of a single cell that does not contain a true nucleus.

Eukaryotes have larger and much more complex cells than do prokaryotes. Eukaryotes traditionally have been divided into four kingdoms: Protista, Fungi, Animalia, and Plantae. Scientists distinguish between these kingdoms based on differences in the structure of the eukaryotes' cells and tissues.

Most members of the kingdom Protista have only one cell. The protists called

Plant cell walls contain cellulose, which makes tree trunks rigid. Shutterstock.com

PARTS OF A TYPICAL PLANT CELL

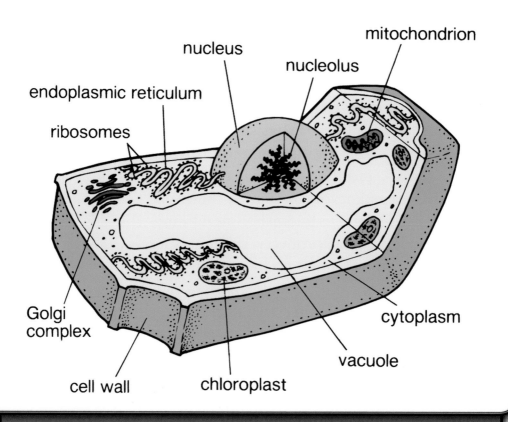

Like animal cells, plant cells have an outer membrane, cytoplasm containing various structures, and a nucleus. Plant cells also have a cell wall, unlike animal cells. **Encyclopædia Britannica, Inc.**

protozoans do not carry out photosynthesis and must obtain their food from other life-forms. Protists known as algae contain chlorophyll and are able to synthesize their food from light energy. Most algae are

CHLOROPHYLL: AN ESSENTIAL PIGMENT

Chlorophyll helps green plants and other organisms with the job of photosynthesis, and it is one of the most important pigments in nature. Photosynthesis is the process by which the radiant energy of sunlight is converted to chemical energy through the synthesis of organic compounds. Chlorophyll is found in virtually all photosynthetic organisms, including green plants, prokaryotic blue-green algae (cyanobacteria), and eukaryotic algae. It absorbs energy from light, and this energy is then used to convert carbon dioxide to carbohydrates.

Chlorophyll occurs in several distinct forms: chlorophylls a and b are the major types found in higher plants and green algae; chlorophylls c and d are found, often with a, in different algae; chlorophyll e is a rare type found in some golden algae; and bacteriochlorophyll occurs in certain photosynthetic bacteria. In green plants chlorophyll occurs in disklike units (thylakoids) in organelles called chloroplasts. The chlorophyll molecule consists of a central magnesium atom surrounded by a nitrogen-containing structure called a porphyrin ring. Attached to the ring is a long carbon–hydrogen side chain, known as a phytol chain. A pigment much like chlorophyll was probably the first step in the evolution of self-sustaining life.

single-celled organisms, but some, such as red, brown, and certain types of green algae, are multicellular. Certain species of multicellular green algae that live in ponds have many plantlike features and are closely related to plants.

Fungi, such as yeasts, molds, and mushrooms, have a cell wall and reproduce by means of spores. Fungi do not contain

Fungi like mushrooms do not contain chlorophyll. Shutterstock.com

chlorophyll, however, and the chemical makeup of the cell walls of fungi is quite different from that of plants. Patterns of reproduction in fungi are also quite different from those of plants.

Animals (kingdom Animalia) are distinguished from protozoa because animals are composed of many cells arranged into tissues. Animal cells lack cell walls and chloroplasts, and they are generally capable of moving about under their own power.

Plants, unlike many animals and protozoans, cannot move about freely by their own efforts. Plants are capable of certain kinds of movement, such as turning toward light and reaching toward water, but not of moving themselves from place to place.

CHAPTER 2

PLANT CLASSIFICATION

Plants may be organized according to the forms in which they grow. They can also be classified according to the length of their life cycles or in terms of their complexity and evolutionary ancestry.

CLASSIFICATION BY GROWTH FORM

A common classification scheme is based on growth form. Plants are called trees if they have tall, woody stems, or trunks, and are generally 8 feet (2.4 meters) or more in height when mature. Shrubs are low, woody plants, usually with many stems branching off close to the ground. Herbs have tender, juicy stems in which the woody tissue is much less developed than it is in shrubs and trees.

Within each of these groups there is a great deal of variety. For example, some trees, such as the giant sequoia, can grow to heights of more than 300 feet (90 meters), whereas others, such as the flowering dogwood, rarely grow to more than 30 feet (9 meters) in height.

The giant sequoia called the General Grant tree (center) *is among the world's largest trees in total bulk. It grows in Kings Canyon National Park in the U.S. state of California.* Bruce Coleman Inc.

The French marigold, a common garden flower, is an annual plant, meaning that it completes its life cycle within one year. Robert Bornemann/Photo Researchers

CLASSIFICATION OF FLOWERING PLANTS

Flowering plants may be divided into three groups, according to the length and pattern of their life cycles. Annuals complete their life cycle in a single year. The seeds sprout, or germinate, the seedlings develop into flowering plants, new seeds are produced, and the parent plant dies—all in a single growing season. Annual plants often grow in habitats that are inhospitable during part of

Tulips are perennial plants, meaning that they live for more than two years. © Corbis

the year. They survive through these inhospitable periods in the form of seeds, which can withstand environmental extremes. Many familiar garden flowers are annuals.

Biennials require two years to complete their life cycle. In the first year they produce stems and leaves. In the second year they produce blossoms and seeds and then die. During the first year they produce through

The agave plant known as American aloe can live for decades before producing one tall flower. **Hemera/Thinkstock**

photosynthesis the food reserves that they need to produce their flowers and seeds the following year. In this group are many garden flowers, including Canterbury bells, foxgloves, hollyhocks, and English daisies.

Perennials live for more than two years. The oldest living thing on Earth is thought to be a bristlecone pine that is about 4,900 years old. Wildflowers are perennial plants. All the common garden perennials, including peonies, irises, and phlox, were developed from wild species.

Some perennials produce flowers and seeds throughout their lives. Others, however, produce flowers only once and then die. The American aloe, or century plant, for example, is a type of agave that typically lives for more than a decade while its stem and leaves grow. Eventually, the plant produces an enormous flowering stalk up to 40 feet (12 meters) tall. The plant dies soon after the flowers mature and seeds are produced.

Most perennials are annual aboveground—that is, their stems, leaves, and blossoms die in the fall. These plants, however, survive through the winter by means of their underground roots and stems. Trees, shrubs, and herbs also live and grow in much the same way.

GARDEN FLOWERS

All the familiar garden flowers of today have been developed from wild flowers. They were chosen for cultivation because of their beauty. By careful selection and cross-pollination of the finest plants, their blooms have been made even more beautiful. Some of them now bear little resemblance to their wild ancestors.

About 10,000 species of plants are cultivated for their ornamental flowers alone. Almost all the countries of the world have contributed to the modern garden. The hollyhock has come from China. It still escapes from gardens and grows wild along railroad embankments and other sunny places where it is undisturbed. Japan is the home of the wisteria and chrysanthemum.

The wild tulip blooms from the Mediterranean eastward into Asia. Turkish gardeners were the first to collect fine specimens and develop the garden tulip. The crocus grows wild in the Alpine meadows of Switzerland, and the foxglove is abundant in English fields. Tropical Africa is the origin of many well-loved flowers. Among them are the gladiolus, geranium, and African violet.

The Oriental poppy grows wild in Iran. The strawflower, bottle brush, and crape myrtle have come from Australia. South America is the home of the petunia, fuchsia, verbena, scarlet sage, spiderflower, nasturtium, and canna. Mexico has contributed the zinnia, marigold, dahlia, and poinsettia.

CLASSIFICATION BY COMPLEXITY

Scientists organize the plant kingdom into divisions that are arranged in order from the simplest to the most complex. The plant divisions can be arranged into three main groups on the basis of differences in the structure of the plant bodies. These groups are the nonvascular plants (liverworts, hornworts, and mosses), seedless vascular plants (ferns and their relatives), and vascular seed plants.

LIVERWORTS, HORNWORTS, AND MOSSES

The first land plants were the liverworts (division Hepatophyta), hornworts (division Anthocerotophyta), and mosses (division Bryophyta). These nonvascular land plants first grew more than 450 million years ago. Plants belonging to these three divisions are able to grow on land and are more complex than most algae. However, they lack the specialized tissues for transporting water and food that are found in more developed plants, and they do not make seeds. Some liverworts, hornworts, and mosses can survive in dry habitats, but they all require abundant moisture to reproduce.

27

Liverworts have simple stems, or none at all, and have either simple leaves or flat green bodies that resemble leaves. On their undersurfaces are rootlike structures but no true roots. Hornworts have small green bodies that are flat and almost circular. The spore cases are erect, slender capsules that rise slightly above the surface of the plants — these are the "horns" of the hornworts. Mosses show the beginnings of leaves, stems, and roots. They were the first green plants to stand erect.

FERNS AND THEIR RELATIVES

Seedless vascular plants—ferns and their relatives—are plants that have specialized tissues for conducting water and food but that do not use seeds to reproduce. They first appeared on dry land more than 400 million years ago. Seedless vascular plants include the club mosses (division Lycophyta) and horsetails and ferns (division Pterophyta). These plants have stems, roots, and leaves that are similar to those of higher plants. They do not produce flowers, however; they reproduce by means of spores. Their vascular tissues allow them to survive in habitats that are sometimes dry but, like the nonvascular

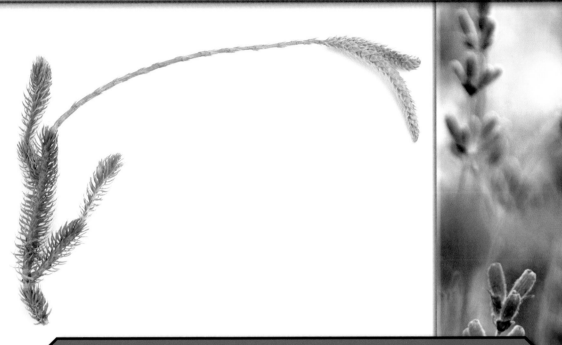

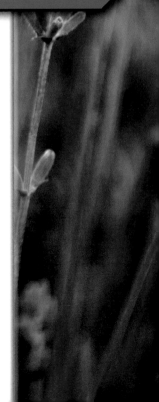

Unlike seed-producing pinecones, the cones at the end of club moss branches produce spores. Neil Fletcher & Matthew Ward/Dorling Kindersley/Getty Images

land plants, they need plenty of moisture to reproduce.

Club mosses are usually a few inches high, though their stems may creep along the ground for distances of more than 50 feet (15 meters). They have slender, simple or branching stems and small scalelike leaves. Club mosses look like little pine trees, with tiny club-shaped "cones" at the tips of the branches. Pine-tree cones, however, produce

29

seeds; the cones of the club mosses produce spores. Horsetails have jointed stems that look somewhat like bamboo. The scaly leaves grow in whorls around the stem at the joints. Like the club mosses, the horsetails have spore-producing cones at the tops of their branches.

Millions of years ago, the ancestors of the modern ferns covered Earth in vast forests. Their remains formed the coal beds found in the ground today. Tropical ferns still grow as tall as trees; however, in temperate climates, ferns are generally small, shade-loving plants.

VASCULAR SEED PLANTS

Vascular seed plants, which include conifers and flowering plants, have transport tissues and produce seeds. Seed plants evolved more than 300 million years ago. Plants that reproduce by way of seeds do not necessarily require abundant moisture to complete their life cycle. As a result, seed plants are able to grow in much drier habitats than are plants that depend on spores for reproduction. Seed plants include five divisions: cycads (Cycadophyta), ginkgo (Ginkgophyta), conifers (Coniferophyta), gnetophytes (Gnetophyta), and flowering

Cycads such as Cycas revoluta *are the most primitive plants that reproduce by means of seeds.* **Courtesy of Knut Norstog**

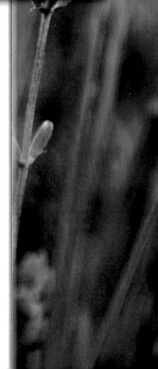

plants (Anthophyta). The first four groups are often called gymnosperms, a name that refers to the fact that their seeds lie naked, or exposed, on the scales of cones. Flowering plants are often called angiosperms—their seeds are protected inside a fruit.

About 280 to 70 million years ago, cycads were among the most abundant plants on Earth. Today they are found only in wet tropical forests. These plants resemble

palm trees. The ginkgo, or maidenhair tree, is often called a living fossil. It is the only surviving species of the Ginkgophyta division. Though native to China, it has been planted as an ornamental tree in many parts of the world.

Conifers are common members of the world's temperate forest ecosystems. Most conifers produce pollen and bear their seeds in cones. These cones vary in size from less than 0.5 inch (1.3 centimeters) in diameter in junipers to nearly 2 feet (0.6 meter) long in sugar pines. Most conifers are evergreen, retaining their needlelike leaves year-round. Several species, however, such as the larch and bald cypress, shed their needles during the harsh winter months. Some conifers, such as the yellowwood of the Southern Hemisphere, have broad leaves. Gnetophytes have many structural features that resemble those of flowering plants, but they have naked seeds.

The Anthophyta first appeared several million years after the first conifers. The reproductive structures of these plants are flowers, and their seeds are protected within a fruit. The Anthophytes are the most abundant of all plants: more than 300,000 species of flowering plants have

THE DURABLE GINKGO TREE

The scientific name of the ginkgo tree is *Ginkgo biloba*. The species is the only surviving member of the order Ginkoales, which is composed of the family Ginkgoaceae. The family dates back to the Permian period of the Paleozoic Era, approximately 286 to 245 million years ago.

Native to China, the ginkgo, also known as the maidenhair tree, has been planted since ancient times in Chinese and Japanese temple gardens. Horticulturists are not sure whether uncultivated groups of ginkgos exist in the wild anymore. The ginkgo is valued in many parts of the world as a beautiful tree that is resistant to fungus and insects. The foliage of the ginkgo is shaped like a pyramid. The tree may reach a height of about 120 feet (37 meters). The column-shaped trunk is sparsely branched. The fan-shaped leathery leaves grow to about 3 inches (8 centimeters) long and 6 inches (15 centimeters) wide. The leaves are divided in the middle by a central notch.

Ginkgo trees are either male or female. The flowers of the male tree produce reproductive cells that are carried to the female trees by the wind. When fully developed, the yellowish plumlike seeds produced by the female tree have an offensive odor.

been described, more than all other kinds of plants combined.

The flowering plants may be divided into the monocotyledons (or monocots) and dicotyledons (or dicots). The sprouting seeds of monocots produce a single embryonic leaf. Those of the dicots produce two embryonic leaves. These two groups are

The lily is an herb called a monocot. Shutterstock.com

distinguished by a number of other features as well, including the number of flower parts, the arrangement of stem tissue, and the pattern of veins in the leaves. Most monocots are herbs; they include such plants as grasses, lilies, and orchids. Not all monocotyledons are small. The palms, for example, may grow to more than 100 feet (30 meters) in height. Dicots include a wide variety of herbs, shrubs, and trees.

CHAPTER 3

PLANT CELLS AND TISSUES

All living things are made up of tiny units called cells, which are composed of organic substances such as carbohydrates, proteins, and fats. In plants, cells are grouped together to form tissues. Plant tissues are said to be simple if they are composed of a single type of cell and complex if they are composed of two or more cell types. The tissues make up the various parts of a plant and perform particular functions.

SIMPLE TISSUES

Also referred to as ground tissues, simple tissues include the tissues known as parenchyma, collenchyma, and sclerenchyma. Parenchyma tissue is composed of parenchyma cells, which are found throughout the plant. They are particularly abundant in the stems and roots. The leaf cells that carry out photosynthesis are also parenchyma cells. Unlike many other plant cells, parenchyma cells are alive at maturity and retain the ability to divide. They perform many functions. Some are specialized for photosynthesis,

THE THREE BASIC TYPES OF PLANT TISSUE

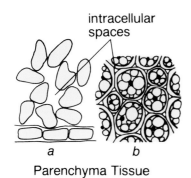

intracellular
spaces

a   *b*

Parenchyma Tissue

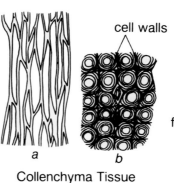

cell walls

a   *b*

Collenchyma Tissue

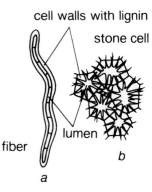

cell walls with lignin

stone cell

fiber

lumen

a   *b*

Sclerenchyma Tissue

a lengthwise
b cross section

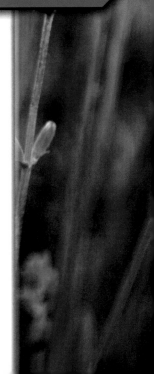

> *Parenchyma tissue makes up most of the pith and cortex of trees, the photosynthetic tissue in leaves, the pulp of fruits, and the endosperm of many seeds. Collenchyma cells chiefly form supporting tissue and are mainly found in the cortex of stems and in leaves. The major function of sclerenchyma is support. Unlike collenchyma, mature cells of this tissue are generally dead and have thick walls containing lignin. Their size, shape, and structure vary greatly.* **Encyclopædia Britannica, Inc.**

others for storage, and still others for secretion and transport. An important class of parenchyma cells makes growth tissues called meristem and cambium. These tissues give rise to all other tissues in the plant body.

Like parenchyma cells, collenchyma cells are alive at maturity. They differ from parenchyma cells in that they have thick cell walls. Collenchyma tissue is most often found in

37

the form of strands or cylinders of cells in stems and leaves. The thick cell walls of collenchyma cells provide support to these plant structures. The strands of tissue in celery are collenchyma tissues.

Sclerenchyma tissue is found throughout the plant. The cells of this tissue also have thick cell walls. These walls are often composed of the substance lignin, which gives the walls a

The grainy consistency of the pear comes from sclereids, or stone cells, scattered throughout the fruit. Shutterstock.com

great deal of strength. At maturity the cells die, but their cell walls remain intact. Sclerenchyma cells give plant parts strength and support.

The most common kinds of sclerenchyma cells are fibers—long slender cells that often occur in bundles or strands. These cells are interwoven so that the tissue is quite strong. Manila hemp, used for making rope, is derived mainly from these fibers. Other sclerenchyma cells, called sclereids, or stone cells, form the shells and husks of seeds and nuts. Stone cells are scattered throughout certain fruits. They give fruits such as pears a gritty texture.

COMPLEX TISSUES

The complex tissues include the dermal and vascular tissues of plants. The epidermis is the outermost layer of cells on the plant body. It covers the leaves, stems, and roots, as well as the flower parts and seeds. In most plants the epidermis is only one cell-layer thick. The epidermal cells are closely packed. When viewed through a microscope, they resemble a stone pavement. The outer cell wall of the epidermis—the cuticle—is particularly thick. It contains a waxy chemical known as cutin. Because water does not easily move through the cuticle, this layer protects the plant from

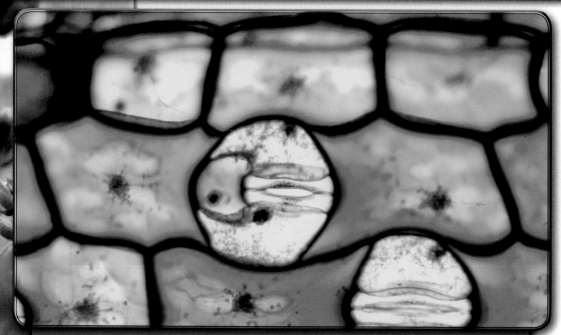

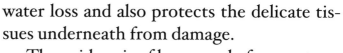

The epidermis of leaves and certain stems contain small openings called stomata, which allow gasses in and out. **Dr. John D. Cunningham/ Visuals Unlimited/Getty Images**

water loss and also protects the delicate tissues underneath from damage.

The epidermis of leaves and of some stems has small openings that allow gases to move in and out. These openings are called stomata (a single opening is called a stoma). Each stoma is opened and closed by two specialized cells called guard cells. Unlike other dermal cells, guard cells have chlorophyll and carry out photosynthesis. These cells swell during the day, causing the stoma to open. During the night they lose pressure, and the stoma closes.

In older stems and roots, the epidermis may be replaced by periderm tissue. Periderm is what produces the tough bark that protects tree trunks. It consists mainly of cork tissue rich in sclerenchyma cells. Periderm also includes specialized parenchyma cells that produce cork tissue by means of cell division.

Inside View of a Root

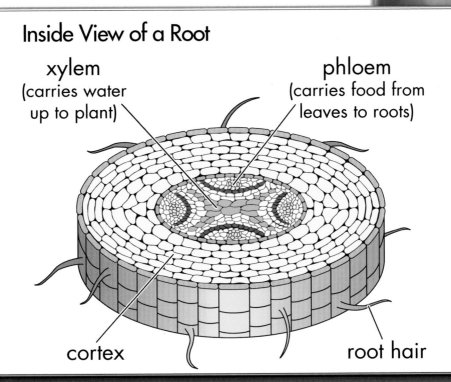

xylem
(carries water
up to plant)

phloem
(carries food from
leaves to roots)

cortex

root hair

A cross section of a typical root of a flowering plant shows the primary xylem and phloem arranged in a central cylinder. **Encyclopædia Britannica, Inc.**

THE TRANSPORT TISSUES: XYLEM AND PHLOEM

Xylem is the principal material in wood. It includes four types of cells: parenchyma, fibers, tracheids, and vessel members. Parenchyma cells are the only living cells in xylem. They form rays through the xylem and transport materials across it. Parenchyma cells also produce other xylem cells. The thick cell walls of fibers provide support to the xylem.

Tracheids are long cigar-shaped cells. They have thick cell walls that contain lignin. Like fibers, they are dead at maturity. The cell walls of tracheids contain many pores, which allow water to flow easily from one tracheid to the next. Tracheids also provide support to the xylem. Tracheids are the only type of water-conducting cells found in such primitive vascular plants as ferns and conifers.

In flowering plants, the cells called vessel members form vessels that run up and down the xylem. Like those of tracheid cells, the cell walls of vessel members contain lignin. As vessel members mature, the cell wall at each end of the cell dissolves and the living part of the cell dies, leaving a continuous "pipe" through which water can move.

Like xylem, phloem includes parenchyma and sclerenchyma cells. Phloem conducts food through the plant body. The type of cell primarily responsible for transporting food through the plant body is the sieve cell. These are elongated cells joined together end to end to form a sieve tube. A vascular bundle may contain hundreds of sieve tubes. Sieve cells are alive at maturity (the transport of food materials requires the activity of living cells). The walls at the ends of sieve cells have large pores through which food materials can be readily moved. The sieve cells of flowering plants lack a nucleus. Adjacent to each sieve cell are several companion cells that function in place of the missing nucleus.

Vascular tissues are specialized for the transport of materials throughout the plant body. They include two types of complex tissue: xylem, which carries water and dissolved minerals, and phloem, which carries food in the form of sugary sap. These complex tissues are arranged either in strands or in units called vascular bundles. The strands form a continuous transport system that extends from the roots, up the stems, to the leaves. The leaf veins are composed of vascular bundles.

Chapter 4

Parts of Plants

A plant is actually more complex than it might appear. Its various parts, composed of specialized cells and tissues, work together to carry on the plant's life functions. The leaves gather sunlight and help the plant make its food; the stems support the plant; the roots anchor the plant and draw water and minerals from the soil; the flowers, fruits, and seeds play a role in the plant's reproduction.

Leaves

Plants may well be thought of as food factories. The most important part of the plant factory is the chemical laboratory—the leaves. Within the cells of the leaves the chlorophyll-containing organelles called chloroplasts carry out photosynthesis. Life on Earth depends on photosynthesis. Without it there would be no green plants, and without green plants there would be no terrestrial animal life.

Although some plants have chloroplasts in stem-tissue cells, green leaves are the chief

The veins of a plant leaf carry water, dissolved minerals, and sugars to and from the leaf tissues. © **Corbis**

laboratories in which photosynthesis takes place. The epidermis of the leaf usually consists of a single layer of cells covering both the top and bottom of the leaf. Most epidermal cells do not contain chloroplasts. The tiny openings called stomata usually occur on the lower surface of the leaf. Stomata permit gases to enter the leaf and allow gases and water vapor to leave. If the stomata were on

the side of the leaf exposed to sunlight, the leaf would lose too much water. Some leaves have chloroplasts and stomata on both sides and turn their edges to the Sun.

Between the upper and lower epidermis of the leaf is a layer of cells called the mesophyll. The mesophyll is composed of parenchyma cells that have chloroplasts. Most photosynthesis takes place in the mesophyll. Mesophyll cells form a loose network with many gaps, allowing carbon dioxide and water vapor to move freely among the cells. A single square inch (6.5 square centimeters) of an elm leaf may have 250 million chloroplasts, and a mature elm tree may have 100,000 leaves.

The veins of the leaves contain the transport tissues—xylem and phloem. Xylem brings water and mineral nutrients such as nitrogen to the mesophyll cells. Phloem transports sugars and organic matter from the mesophyll cells to other parts of the plant.

The colorless plants that lack chlorophyll are either parasites, which live on other plants, or saprophytes, which live on decaying animal or vegetable matter. Dodder, mistletoe, and Indian pipe are parasites.

Indian pipe is a type of parasite. **Panoramic Images/Getty Images**

STEMS

A crucial part of higher plants is the stem. (The simplest plants have none.) Stems give the plant support. Leaves, flowers, and branches develop from buds on the stem.

Stems have many different forms. The woody upright trunk of a tree is a stem. Shrubs have many woody stems. Lianas are species of large vines that have climbing stems with roots in the ground. Grapevines are woody lianas. The stems of such plants may also have curly tendrils—modified branches that cling to a tree or other support. In tropical forests there are many kinds of woody lianas that climb up the trunks of trees into the sunlight.

The stems of herbs have scarcely any woody tissue. The banana tree is not a tree at all but an herb because its trunk, or stem, is not woody. There are several kinds of herbaceous stems. Most of the familiar flowers have upright stems. The stems of cucumber and pumpkin plants lie prostrate on the ground. Morning-glory and bindweed stems twine upward with the help of tendrils.

A horizontal stem growing below the surface of the ground is called a rhizome. The common iris, for example, grows from a rhizome. Short, fleshy underground stems are

THREE STAGES OF STEM GROWTH

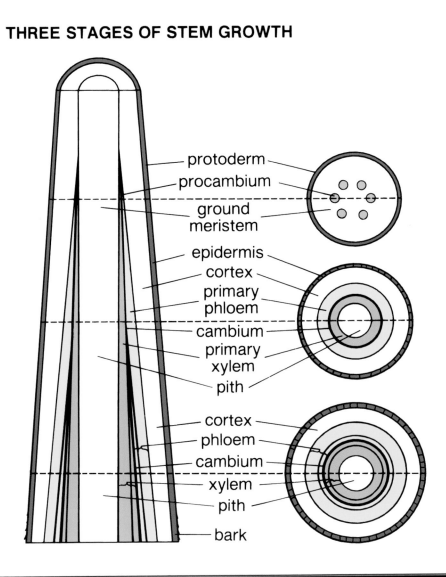

- protoderm
- procambium
- ground meristem
- epidermis
- cortex
- primary phloem
- cambium
- primary xylem
- pith
- cortex
- phloem
- cambium
- xylem
- pith
- bark

A longitudinal section, left, and cross section, right, of a growing stem show the organization of various tissues for younger (top) and older (bottom) parts of the stem. **Encyclopædia Britannica, Inc.**

called tubers. The potato is a tuber. Its "eyes" are actually buds from which the aboveground potato stems sprout. Upright underground stems enlarged with stored food, such as those produced by the gladiolus, are called corms. A stem that grows erect and then curves over, touching the ground at its tip, is called a stolon. Certain roses and rasp-berries have stoloniferous, or stolon-bearing, stems. A stem that runs along the ground, often far from the point where the plant has its roots, is called a runner. Strawberry plants have such stems.

Flowering plants may be classified as monocots and dicots not only on the basis of the formation of their embryonic leaves, but also on the basis of the arrangement of the vascular bundles within their stems. In dicots, or plants with two seed leaves, the bundles are arranged in a circle around the central portion of the stem, called the pith. Beans and most trees and shrubs are dicots. One way to recognize dicots is

Potatoes are the fleshy, underground stems of the potato plant. **Grant Heilman Photography**

Beans can be identified as dicots by the veining in their leaves. **De Agostini Picture Library/Getty Images**

by the veining of their leaves: the veins of most dicots are arranged in the form of a network.

A tree trunk is a typical dicot stem. The stump of a tree reveals the same kind of rings as those in the stem of a violet viewed under a microscope. Immediately beneath the outer layer, or epidermis, of the dicot stem is a layer called the cortex. The cortex is composed of parenchyma cells that primarily store food. Inside the cortex are the vascular bundles. The phloem, which conducts food through the plant body, is located within the vascular bundles toward the outside of the stem. The xylem, toward the inside of the stem, conducts water upward from the roots. Between the xylem and the phloem is the third tissue, the cambium. This is a layer of parenchyma cells; the cells toward the outside produce phloem cells, and those toward the inside produce xylem cells. The growth in the diameter of a stem takes place in the cambium layer. The center of the stem, the pith, serves as a storage place for reserve food.

In woody dicots, such as shrubs and trees, the cambium forms a continuous ring around the stem and produces a continuous ring of phloem to the outside and xylem to the inside. As a result, the xylem forms a solid core—the wood. As the stem matures, the pith and cortex may disappear. The cell walls of the tracheid cells and vessel members of the xylem that are produced in the spring-time are thinner than those produced in the summer. This variation results in the forma-tion of distinct rings in the wood that indi-cate the growth pattern of the tree over the period of a year. These rings are called annual rings.

In monocots, which have one embryonic leaf, vascular bundles in the form of strands are scat-tered throughout the stem. The veins in their leaves generally run par-allel to one another. Grasses, corn (maize), bananas, palms, and lilies are among the monocots.

Green bananas. Shutterstock.com

Plant Buds

Stems are distinguished from roots in that stems have buds. Buds called terminal buds occur at the tip of the stem and lateral buds grow on the sides of the stem. The buds develop into leaves, side branches, and flowers or cones. Annuals, most biennials, and a few perennials have naked buds that are covered only by the flower parts or elementary leaves. Perennials that must survive the hardships of winter have protected buds that are covered with waterproof waxy bud scales. When the buds begin to swell in the spring, the bud scales fall off, leaving scars. The amount of annual growth of a plant can be measured by the distance between these scars.

Active buds are those that are growing and producing new plant parts. Most buds are latent—that is, they do not grow unless the plant suffers injury, as from fire, insects, or frost. Latent buds lie in reserve and are stimulated to growth only when necessary to restore the plant to good health.

Monocot stems have a cortex and vascular bundles with xylem and phloem. Their vascular bundles do not have a cambium layer, and the stems have no central pith. Because they

lack cambium, monocots grow in height but, with the exception of palms, the diameter of their stems does not increase.

Vascular bundles divide into smaller bundles as they enter branches, twigs, leafstalks, and finally leaves. Food moves not only up and down but also sideways into all parts of the plant. Vascular rays and pith rays carry sap horizontally through the cell walls.

Roots

The roots may be called the receiving rooms of the plant factory, for one of their chief functions is to draw water and minerals from the soil. As rainwater filters into the ground, it dissolves the minerals in the soil. The plant uses this solution for its work in making food. Roots also anchor the plant in the soil and serve as places to store food.

When a seed sprouts, the first thing to break out of the coat is the root (called the radicle at this early stage). No matter what the position of the seed is when it is planted—whether upright, sideways, or upside down—the root always turns downward.

The most important part of a root is its tip, where the actively dividing cells in the

PARTS OF A ROOT TIP

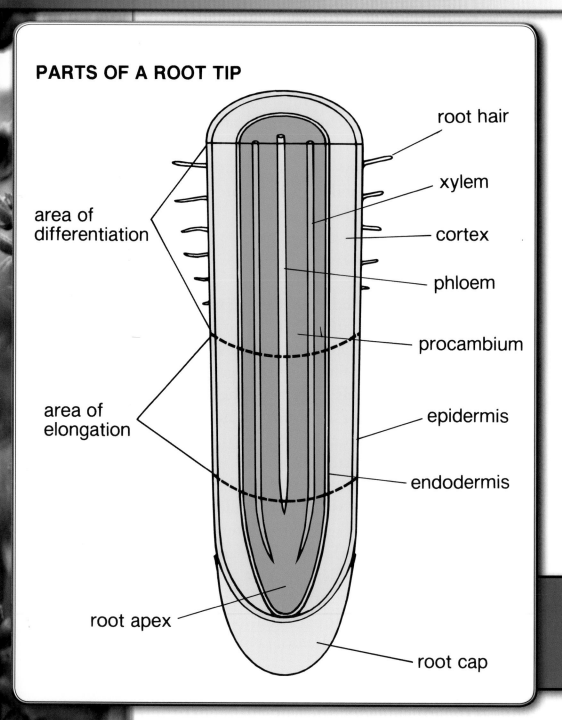

area of differentiation

area of elongation

root apex

root hair

xylem

cortex

phloem

procambium

epidermis

endodermis

root cap

meristem tissues are found. Just above the very end of the root, called the root cap, root hairs extend from the cells of the epidermis. These root hairs increase the surface area in contact with the soil and increase the plant's ability to draw water and minerals. The root hairs are seldom seen because when a plant is pulled up they are broken off. This is why flowers and trees that are to be transplanted must be carefully dug up, with a ball of earth to which the roots are fastened remaining at the base.

Roots take in enormous quantities of water. It has been estimated that one alfalfa plant requires about 900 pounds (408 kilograms) of water; a potato plant, 636 pounds (288 kilograms); wheat, 500 pounds (227 kilograms); and cactus, 40 pounds (18 kilograms). A small amount of this water is used for photosynthesis or is retained in the plant's cells. Most water passes into the air through the leaves in a process called transpiration. Because wall this water must enter the plant through its roots, a plant

In a growing root tip, cells in the root apex divide and produce new cells for the root. The new cells grow in the area of elongation and mature in the area of differentiation. **Encyclopædia Britannica, Inc.**

must have a vast root network. After four months, a single rye plant, for example, has about 13,800,000 roots. If the epidermis of those roots was spread out flat, it would cover a football field.

FLOWERS AND FRUITS

Flowers are the primary reproductive organs of those plants belonging to the division Anthophyta. The flowers are where the seeds that will give rise to new plants are produced. The primary parts of the flower are the sepals, petals, stamens, and pistil.

The leaflike sepals form the protective covering for the flower bud before it opens. All of the petals together are called the corolla. The petals are often brightly colored to attract insects or other animals that might pollinate the flower. Some flowers have glands at the base of the petals or sepals that produce nectar—an additional attraction to pollinators.

The stamens produce pollen grains. In a typical flower the lowermost portion of the pistil is swollen to form the ovary, within which the ovules are found. Ovules develop into seeds after they are fertilized—that is,

Pollen moves up the stamen to the pistil. Shutterstock.com

after pollen is transferred from the stamen to the pistil.

The arrangement of flower parts varies from one plant species to another. Often the color and shape of the corolla is such that only particular insects or hummingbirds are attracted to the flower. For example, only insects with long "tongues" can reach the nectar produced

at the base of the corolla of certain orchids. Some flowers lack sepals, petals, or both. This is true, for example, of many forest trees that depend on wind, rather than insects, to carry pollen from flower to flower. In some plants, flowers may be specialized: some have stamens and others have pistils. The common persimmon of temperate forests, for example, has "male" trees, which produce flowers that have only stamens, and "female" trees, which produce flowers that have only pistils.

After the ovules in the ovary have been fertilized, the ovary may begin to enlarge into a fruit. A fruit is a matured ovary that contains seeds. In some plants the ovary wall may separate into two layers. The inner layer forms a hard shell, called the stone or pit, that encloses the seed. The outer layer may be fleshy and succulent. The peach, cherry, and apricot are examples of such fruits. In the fruits called berries, the seeds are embedded entirely in fleshy tissue. Dry fruits, such as nuts and acorns, are those in which the ovary wall forms a hard outer covering.

SEEDS

Embryonic plants, called seeds, vary considerably in size. Orchids, for example, produce seeds as small as dust particles. The coconut is one of the largest seeds in the plant kingdom. In many seeds, the protective outer seed coat is composed of sclerenchyma cells, which make the coat resistant to physical damage and which may also contain waxes and oils that help prevent water loss.

Coconuts are among the biggest seeds in the plant kingdom. picturegarden/Digital Vision/Getty Images

The embryo within the seed begins as a single cell, the zygote (a fertilized egg). The basic organs of the plant body can be found in the embryo. In some seeds the embryonic leaves, or cotyledons, are quite large, filling most of the volume of the seed. Such cotyledons are major sources of stored food for the embryo. Beans are examples of plants with large cotyledons. In many other plants the cotyledons are relatively small, and the embryo is nourished by a tissue called endosperm.

CHAPTER 5

USES OF PLANTS

Human beings depend on plants. Directly or indirectly, plants provide food, clothing, fuel, shelter, and many other necessities of life. Humankind's dependence on crops such as wheat and corn (maize) is obvious, but without grass and grain the livestock that provide people with food and other animal products could not survive either.

FOOD

The food that plants store for their own growth is also the food that humans and other organisms need to live. In North America the chief food plants are cereal grains. (The word cereal comes from Ceres, the Roman goddess of agriculture.) Major cereal crops include corn (maize), wheat, oats, rice, barley, and rye. Legumes are the second greatest source of food from plants. Legumes such as peas, dry beans, soybeans, and peanuts are high in protein and oil. Sago, taro, and cassava are major starchy foods in certain tropical parts of the world. (Seaweeds, an important part of

Wheat, a member of the grass family, is one of the oldest and most important of the cereal crops. **Robert Glusic/Getty Images**

the diet in some cultures, especially in Asia, are not actually plants but rather are a form of algae.)

Seasonings are derived from plant materials. People have used herbs and spices for

64

Cinnamon and ginger are spices that come from plant stems.
iStockphoto/Thinkstock

centuries to flavor and preserve food. Some seasonings, such as pepper and nutmeg, are obtained from dried fruits. Others, including thyme, sage, and rosemary, come from leaves. Plant stems provide such spices as ginger and cinnamon.

GRAINS

Members of the grass family that yield starchy seeds suitable for food are called grains. Grains are also known as cereal, or cereal grains. The grains most commonly cultivated are barley, corn (maize), millet, oats, rice, rye, sorghum, and wheat.

As human food, cereals are usually sold in their raw grain form—though some are frozen or canned—or used as ingredients in various food products. As animal feed, they are consumed mainly by livestock and poultry, which are eventually consumed by humans as meat, dairy, and poultry products. Grains are also used industrially in the production of a wide range of substances, including glucose and alcohols.

Many beverages are derived from plants. Coffee, tea, and cocoa are prepared by steeping plant material in hot water. Other drinks are "ready-made" by nature: orange, lemon, and grape juice; coconut milk; apple cider; and apricot nectar are examples. Some beverages come from processed plant materials.

Clothing

Much human clothing is made from material that comes directly from plants. Cotton is the principal plant used for clothing manufacture. Artificial textile fibers, such as rayon, are manufactured chiefly from cellulose, which is found mainly in the cell walls of plants. Linen is obtained from the flax plant. In addition, plants once furnished most of the dyestuffs with which cloth was colored.

Paper

More than 4,500 years ago, the ancient Egyptians prepared the first paper from the fibrous stems of papyrus, a grasslike plant. It is from the name of this plant that the word paper is derived. In about AD 100 the Chinese invented a method of manufacturing paper that is still used today. Plant fibers are placed in water and reduced to a pulp. The water is sieved off, and the pulp is pressed and dried to yield a thin sheet of paper. Nearly any plant material that is rich in cellulose may be used to make pulp. Today, wood from such trees as pine and aspen is the most widely used source of pulp for paper.

Shelters such as log homes are built from wood in many parts of the world. Shutterstock.com

SHELTER AND VARIOUS PRODUCTS

Shelter in many parts of the world is made from wood. Plant materials appear in a number of places in human dwellings. Furniture

68

is commonly composed of wood and cloth made from plant fibers. Walls are often covered with paper, and some paints and varnishes are derived from plant extracts.

Products made from trees are numerous. They include cork, kapok, rubber, turpentine, gums and resins, and tannins. Trees also yield important fats and oils, such as cocoa butter and tung oil.

Cellulose, found in great abundance in many plant parts, is a basic ingredient of certain plastics and other synthetic substitutes for natural fibers, leather, glass, rubber, jewels, stone, and metal. Corn (maize) and soybeans have numerous industrial uses.

FUEL

Coal and natural gas are fuels used for heating and cooking. Each originated in plants and other organisms that lived on Earth long ago. After the organisms died, their remains became buried deep underground, where compression and heat converted them to fossil fuels. Peat, which is formed from partially decayed plant material buried in bogs, is a common fuel in Ireland and certain other countries.

THE MANY USES
OF ORCHIDS

Orchids are put to a wide variety of uses all around the world. Most vanilla is produced

The orchid species Vanilla planifolia *produces most vanilla.* Shutterstock.com

from one orchid species, *Vanilla planifolia*, although two additional species are also cultivated commercially (*V. pompona* and *V. tahitensis*). The principal vanilla-growing areas are Madagascar, Mexico, French Polynesia, Réunion, Dominica, Indonesia, the West Indies, Seychelles, and Puerto Rico.

Various other orchids are used for folk medicines and cures. In the West Indies, the bulbs of *Bletia purpurea* are boiled, and the liquid is thought to cure poisoning from fish. In Malaysia, women take a drink made from the boiled leaves of *Nervilia aragoana* to prevent sickness after childbirth. In Melaka (formerly Malacca), a state in western Malaysia, boils are treated with a poultice made from the entire plant of *Oberonia anceps*.

Certain orchids are also used for food or food supplements. In Malaysia, the leaves of one species of *Anoectochilus* are sold as a vegetable, and the leaves of *Dendrobium salaccense* are cooked as a seasoning with rice. In certain parts of the Asian tropics, the tubers of some species of *Gastrodia* are eaten like potatoes.

Wood is still burned for heat in many parts of the world, and it is popular for use in open fireplaces. Charcoal, formed from incompletely burned wood, is a major fuel in many tropical countries where other

fuels are unavailable or are very expensive. Charcoal is also popular in North America for outdoor cooking.

MEDICINE

Through the ages, people have found that certain plants could be used to relieve their aches and pains. Most medicine men and physicians in ancient cultures were experts on plants. In fact, the study of botany in Europe and America had its beginnings in medicine, when doctors searched for herbs to cure disease.

Many medicinal plants that were discovered by early peoples are still in use today. For example, some Native Americans chewed on the leaves of willows to relieve aches and pains. These leaves contain salicylic acid, a compound very similar to aspirin. The leaves of the foxglove yield digitalis, which is used to treat heart disease. Quinine, from the bark of the South American cinchona tree, was long used to combat malaria.

Medicinal substances are still being discovered in plants. Vincristine, a medicine that has proved effective in the treatment of leukemia in children, was discovered in the common periwinkle plant. The periwinkle is native to South Africa and is cultivated in gardens around the world. Many plants are invaluable sources of vitamins, whose importance to human growth and health was an important 20th-century discovery.

Not all drugs derived from plants are beneficial. Some plant drugs are violent poisons or habit-forming narcotics. These include peyote, which is derived from a cactus, and opium, which comes from a poppy.

Conclusion

As this volume has detailed, the daily existence of human beings is directly influenced by plants. Plants furnish food and seasonings; raw materials for industry such as wood, oils, and rubber; fibers for the manufacture of fabrics and clothing; medicines; fuels; and pulp for making paper. Much of Earth's population relies on rice, corn (maize), and wheat as their primary source of food. Apart from their commercial and aesthetic value, plants conserve other natural resources by protecting soils from erosion, controlling water levels and quality, and helping to produce a favorable atmosphere.

Biologists continue to study the world's known plant species and examine how the various parts of plants function and how plants should be classified. They also continue to work to identify new plant species and to assess the impact of plants on Earth's ecosystems. Such studies may ultimately result in the discovery of many helpful new uses of plants and lead to a deeper appreciation of the significance of the role that plants play in the maintenance of life on Earth.

biennial Growing vegetatively during the first year and fruiting and dying during the second.

cambium A thin formative layer between the xylem and phloem of most vascular plants that gives rise to new cells and is responsible for secondary growth.

cellulose A complex carbohydrate, or polysaccharide, of glucose units that constitutes the chief part of the cell walls of plants.

chloroplast Structure within a green plant cell in which photosynthesis occurs.

collenchyma A plant tissue that consists of living usually elongated cells with unevenly thickened walls and acts as support especially in areas of primary growth.

conifer Trees and shrubs, most of which are evergreens and have needle-shaped or scaly leaves.

corolla The part of a flower that consists of the separate or fused petals and consti-tutes the inner whorl of the perianth, or floral envelope.

cotyledon The first leaf or one of the first pair or whorl of leaves developed by the embryo of a seed plant or of some lower plants (as ferns).

lignin Complex oxygen-containing organic substance that, with cellulose, forms the chief constituent of wood.

meristem Region of cells capable of division and growth in plants.

organelle A specialized cellular part (as a mitochondrion, lysosome, or ribosome) that is similar to an organ.

parenchyma Tissue typically composed of living cells that are thin-walled, unspecialized in structure, and therefore adaptable, with differentiation, to various functions.

perennial Any plant that persists for several years, usually with new herbaceous growth from a part that survives from season to season.

rhizome Horizontal, underground plant stem capable of producing the shoot and root systems of a new plant.

sepal Lower, or outermost, part of the flower that folds over the tender, closed bud and protects it from cold and other injuries while it is developing.

stoma A microscopic opening or pore in the epidermis of a leaf or young stem.

thylakoid Any of the membranous disks of lamellae within plant chloroplasts that

are composed of protein and lipid and are the sites of the photochemical reactions of photosynthesis.

vascular Of or relating to a channel for the conveyance of a body fluid (as blood of an animal or sap of a plant) or to a system of such channels.

xylem Part of the vascular system that conveys water and dissolved minerals from the roots to the rest of the plant and may also furnish mechanical support.

Botanical Research Institute of
    Texas (BRIT)
500 East 4th Street
Fort Worth, TX 76102
(817) 332-4441
Web site: http://www.brit.org
BRIT is dedicated to increasing public
    understanding of plants and vegeta-
    tion through its research, publications,
    and collections. Its extensive library
    of botanical literature is available to
    the public and educational programs
    are offered for teachers, students, and
    families.

Botanical Society of America (BSA)
4475 Castleman Avenue
St. Louis, MO 63110
(314) 577-9566
Web site: http://www.botany.org
The members of the BSA consist of pro-
    fessionals, academics, and educators
    who seek to share their research inter-
    ests and promote the study of plants
    and related organisms among the public
    through the BSA's publications and out-
    reach programs.

Center for Plant Conservation (CPC)
P.O. Box 299
St. Louis, MO 63166
(314) 577-9450
Web site: http://www.centerforplant
    conservation.org
The CPC is made up of 36 member
    botanical institutions that are dedi-
    cated to conserving plants native to
    the United States and preventing their
    extinction through research and resto-
    ration efforts.

Native Plant Society of British Columbia
    (NPSBC)
Suite 195
1917 West 4th Avenue
Vancouver, BC V6J 1M7
Canada
(604) 831-5069
Web site: http://www.npsbc.org
The NPSBC is centered around the
    study of plants native to the British
    Columbia province. Events for
    members include field trips, work-
    shops, and presentations by guest
    speakers.

UBC Botanical Garden and Centre for
    Plant Research
6804 SW Marine Drive
Vancouver, BC V6T 1Z4
Canada
(604) 822-9666
Web site: http://www.ubcbotanical
    garden.org
The living plant collection at the UBC
    Botanical Garden—the second largest
    in Canada—attracts numerous visitors
    every year and provides the research-
    ers at its associated Centre for Plant
    Research with material for their world-
    class studies in such areas as evolution
    and biodiversity.

United States Botanic Garden
100 Maryland Avenue SW
Washington, DC 20001
(202) 225-8333
Web site: http://www.usbg.gov
The United States Botanic Garden exhib-
    its a wide array of plants from all over
    the world and furthers its mission of
    disseminating knowledge and appre-
    ciation of plants of all types through
    family and educational programs.

WEB SITES

Due to the changing nature of Internet links, Rosen Educational Services has developed an online list of Web sites related to the subject of this book. This site is updated regularly. Please use this link to access the list:

http://www.rosenlinks.com/biol/pcpu

BIBLIOGRAPHY

Ballard, Carol. *Plant Variation and Classification* (Rosen Central, 2010).

Boehm Jerome, Kate. *Plants: Important Producers* (Millmark Education, 2008).

Boothroyd, Jennifer. *Plants and the Environment* (Lerner Publications, 2008).

Claybourne, Anna. *Plant Secrets: Plant Life Processes* (Raintree, 2006).

Fullick, Ann. *Variation and Classification* (Heinemann Library, 2006).

Gibson, J. Phil, and Gibson, Terri R. *Plant Ecology* (Chelsea House, 2006).

Glimn-Lacy, Janice, and Kaufman, Peter B. *Botany Illustrated: Introduction to Plants, Major Groups, Fowering Plant Families*, 2nd ed. (Springer, 2006).

Goodman, Emily, and Limbacher Tildes, Phyllis. *Plant Secrets* (Charlesbridge, 2009).

Greenaway, Theresa. *The Plant Kingdom: A Guide to Plant Classification and Biodiversity* (Raintree Steck-Vaughn, 2000).

Howell, Laura, and others. *World of Plants* (Scholastic, 2003).

Lack, Andrew, and Evans, D.E. *Plant Biology* (Taylor & Francis, 2005).

Llewellyn, Claire. *Plants of the World* (Franklin Watts, 2006).

Rosenbaum, Judith, and Parkes, Brenda. *Plant Parts We Eat* (Newbridge Educational, 2007).

Spilsbury, Richard, and Spilsbury, Louise. *Plant Parts*, rev. ed. (Heinemann Library, 2008).

Sumner, Judith. *The Natural History of Medicinal Plants* (Timber Press, 2000).

Van Wyk, Ben-Erik, and Wink, Michael. *Medicinal Plants of the World: An Illustrated Scientific Guide to Important Medicinal Plants and Their Uses* (Timber Press, 2004).

Wells, Diana. *100 Flowers and How They Got Their Names* (Algonquin Books, 1997).

INDEX